CUNARD

THE MOST FAMOUS OCEAN LINERS IN THE WORLD™

VOGUE ON

ALEXANDER MCQUEEN

Chloe Fox

Quadrille
PUBLISHING

Alexander McQueen photographed by David Bailey for Vogue *in 2002.*

page 1 *From 2009's 'Natural Distinction, Un-Natural Selection' collection, an embroidered minidress, photographed by Lachlan Bailey.*

pages 2-3 *From the same collection, a vertebrae-print suit, photographed by Nick Knight.*

'I WANT TO BE THE PURVEYOR OF A
CERTAIN SILHOUETTE OR A WAY OF
CUTTING SO THAT, WHEN I'M DEAD
AND GONE, PEOPLE WILL KNOW THAT
THE TWENTY-FIRST CENTURY WAS
STARTED BY ALEXANDER MCQUEEN.'

ALEXANDER MCQUEEN

—

FASHION OUTSIDER

In MAY 2011, THE FASHION WORLD GATHERED at the Metropolitan Museum of Art's annual Costume Institute Gala in New York to pay tribute to Alexander McQueen, the late British fashion designer whose work was being celebrated in a retrospective exhibition entitled *Savage Beauty*. At this memorial, his presence was almost tangible: it was in the dresses worn by his friends and models – actresses Salma Hayek, Sarah-Jessica Parker, artist and socialite Daphne Guinness, models Gisele Bundchen, Naomi Campbell and Karen Elson all wore McQueen – and, most of all, inside the exhibition itself. It displayed the signature passions found in his work: exquisite tailoring, historical reference, moulding, slashing and re-shaping, and his concerns with nature, politics and culture. *Savage Beauty* would go on to become one of the Museum's most popular and highly attended exhibitions of all time.

Just five years previously, the man himself had accompanied the actress Sarah Jessica Parker – both dressed in matching McQueen tartan – to *AngloMania: Tradition and Transgression in British Fashion*, another exhibition at the Museum in which his work featured heavily. Alexander 'Lee' McQueen CBE, four-times British Designer of the Year (1996, 1997, 2001, 2003) and Council of Fashion Designers of America International Designer of the Year (2003), stood at the helm of British fashion for fifteen years, and yet he remains something of a paradox. He was a working-class boy with haute couture sensibility, an iconoclast with a reverence for tradition, a shameless self-publicist who couldn't stand the limelight. Like the eerie hologram – now a face, now a silver skull – that adorned the cover of the *Savage Beauty* catalogue, he seems to resist definition. But perhaps of all of the many themes in his work that his restless mind seemed to come back to time and time again, was finding light in the darkness, hope in desolation, beauty in death. From his controversial early collections to the elegiac beauty of his last, McQueen's designs reveal the workings of a truly original mind, an artist and visionary whose legacy would stretch well beyond his life and into the future of fashion.

His extraordinary career took him from humble beginnings as an apprentice on Savile Row to the creative directorship of his own eponymous global brand. His is a story of hard work, ambition and preternatural talent. Much has been made – some might say too much – of McQueen's rags-to-riches rise to fame. Despite having been instrumental in its creation, the designer himself quickly grew impatient with the reductive fable of a cockney yob made good. 'The press started that, not me,' he protested. 'It's the Pygmalion syndrome. It's not true … at the end of the day, you are a good designer or not and it doesn't matter where you came from. I don't think you can become a good designer, or a great designer, or whatever. To me, you just are one. To know about colour, proportion, shape, cut, balance, is part of a gene.'

The youngest of six children, Lee Alexander McQueen was born on 17th March 1969 in Lewisham, south London. When he was less than a year old, the family moved further east, eventually settling in a terraced house in Stratford. His father Ronald, of Scottish descent, drove a black cab (friends remember his youngest son's brilliant back-street knowledge of London's streets). His mother, Joyce, a passionate social historian, stayed at home with her children until Lee was 16, after which she taught evening classes in genealogy. She traced her own family ancestry back 250 years to the French Huguenots, who had fled religious persecution and settled in Spitalfields.

Throughout his career, the designer would draw obsessively on his heritage; he claimed to recall clearly a childhood trip with his mother to the family records centre at St Catherine's House to track their ancestry. After his 1992 Graduation Show from Central Saint Martins College of Art and Design, 'Jack the Ripper Stalks his Victims', Joyce McQueen – who had spent many nights helping her son to prepare for the show – would remember her youngest son's acute boyhood interest in the Victorian serial killer, one of whose victims had been housed in an inn belonging to one of their ancestors. In subsequent collections McQueen would directly allude to his personal genealogy, for example his Scottish forebears in 'Highland Rape' (1995) and 'Widows of

Culloden' (2006) and an ancestor victim of the seventeenth-century Salem witch trials in 'In Memory of Elizabeth Howe, Salem 1692' (2007). In others, the references were more muted, his work mixing elements of a romanticised past and an imagined future.

From a young age, McQueen knew that he would be 'something in fashion'. When he was three years old, he drew his first design, a picture of Cinderella 'with a tiny waist and a huge gown', onto the wall of one of his sisters' bedrooms. 'I always, always wanted to be a designer' recalled the man who, when he was growing up, had a sheet of paper stamped with the words CALVIN KLEIN stuck to his bedroom wall. 'I read books on fashion from the age of twelve, I followed designers' careers. I knew Giorgio Armani was a window dresser, Emanuel Ungaro was a tailor.' The self-proclaimed 'pink sheep of the family' (who first realised he was gay on a family trip to a Pontins holiday camp where he won the 'Prince of Pontins' beauty competition), the young McQueen enjoyed nothing more than advising his three older sisters on what to wear, for everything from job interviews to first dates.

McQueen's attachment to his Scottish heritage, epitomised here in a Tim Walker shoot of designs from his 1998 'Joan' collection for British Vogue, *was a rich vein that ran throughout his career.*

overleaf *A decade on in 2008, a wool tartan dress from his much-lauded 'The Girl Who Lived in a Tree' collection, shows an undiminished preoccupation. Photograph by Venetia Scott.*

Other boyhood interests, beyond fashion, fed into McQueen's adult design aesthetic. He had a passion for birds and was a member of the Young Ornithologists Club of Great Britain, often climbing onto the rooftop of a building near his home to watch kestrels flying overhead; and he loved water – an early interest in synchronised swimming gave way to an adult passion for scuba diving. Plumage, feathering, flight and floating are all trademark motifs which can be found, with varying degrees of subtlety, in his work.

'I like things to be modern and still have a bit of tradition.'

ALEXANDER MCQUEEN

When he was 16 years old, McQueen left school with only one academic qualification – in art. Later that year, after seeing a news feature lamenting the lack of apprentices on Savile Row, Joyce McQueen encouraged her son to apply for a job. Within weeks, he found himself working at Anderson & Sheppard, tailors by appointment to the British Royal Family, under Cornelius 'Con' O'Callaghan, one of the most respected coat makers in the business.

McQueen would recall the stifling atmosphere of a late boyhood spent as a young, gay man working on Savile Row ('the most homophobic people I ever worked with') but he was always the first to acknowledge the value of the skills he learnt there. 'I spent a long time learning how to construct clothes', he would later recall. 'Which is important to do before you can deconstruct them.'

McQueen worked hard, with focused intent, in the time he spent at Anderson & Sheppard. Colleagues remember him as a fast learner, endlessly asking questions of the master tailors and working late into the night, honing his new skills. It paid off; a year earlier than was expected, he had mastered the art of making a 'forward' – the term for a jacket before its sleeves, back lining, buttonholes, top collar and finishing stitches have been completed.

This Cleopatra-style gold dress was a standout piece from his 2007 collection 'In Memory of Elizabeth Howe, Salem 1692'. Howe was an ancestress of McQueen's who was accused of witchcraft. Photograph by Roger Dean.

In 1988, McQueen moved a few doors down Savile Row to Gieves & Hawkes. Here, he worked mainly on military tailoring, acquiring interests and skills that would inform his later work over and over again. But in less than a year, McQueen had grown bored, leaving the position on his 20th birthday in 1989 and moving on to a post at the theatrical costumiers Angels, where he cut clothes for some of the bigger London productions, including *Les Miserables*. Such period costume – especially that worn by women in the nineteenth century – would also become an important influence in McQueen's design. 'He would buy eighteenth-century military coats to study' said the fashion writer Plum Sykes, who met him in 1993 while she was working as an intern at British *Vogue*. 'And he was intrigued by Victorian boning and crinolines.'

'AS A PLACE FOR INSPIRATION, BRITAIN IS THE BEST IN THE WORLD ... YOU'RE INSPIRED BY THE ANARCHY IN THE COUNTRY.'

ALEXANDER MCQUEEN

'I SPENT A LONG TIME LEARNING HOW TO CONSTRUCT CLOTHES, WHICH IS IMPORTANT TO DO BEFORE YOU CAN DECONSTRUCT THEM.'

ALEXANDER MCQUEEN

Only a tailor as masterful as McQueen could have so much fun with the subversion of tradition. It is illustrated in this innovative take on the traditional Dior houndstooth skirt suit, from 'The Horn of Plenty' collection, photographed by Mario Testino in 2009.

previous page *Plumage and patriotism: two of the designer's strongest influences make for a striking Richard Burbridge image of this feather-effect gold silk dress from 2001's 'What a Merry-go-Round'.*

At the heart of McQueen's creative imagination was his technical virtuosity; his shape-altering designs always had an immaculate cut at the core. Speaking of his tailoring, his friend and mentor the late fashion stylist Isabella Blow once said 'Like Rome, he's got fantastic foundations'. Almost more than anything, this high standard of refinement, of craft, was what mattered to McQueen. 'Designer fashion shouldn't be throwaway,' he declared. 'I want to create pieces that can be handed down, like an heirloom. I want people to get joy out of clothes again.' Regularly, McQueen would refer back to the importance of those years spent training on 'The Row'. In one of life's neat acts of serendipity, McQueen had ended up in the best environment in which to nurture his natural talents. 'I remember when I first started out, I used to walk past what was then Valentino on Bond Street and just look in amazement at the way the clothes were finished … It was miraculous, so inspiring.'

A Corinne Day shoot from 2002 encapsulates McQueen's passion for military tailoring, learnt during a year spent working at Gieves and Hawkes in 1998.

Those who worked with McQueen later in his career attest endlessly, and with reverence, to the speed and dexterity with which he could cut a garment. 'He made you feel like you might as well pack your bags and go home' said Sarah Burton, who worked at McQueen's right hand from 1996 until his death fourteen years later. 'He could draw a pattern on the floor; he could change things so confidently. He had a very masculine, instinctive way of doing it. He'd get beads of sweat on his head. His knowledge of clothes, of what he wanted, was so black and white. There were no grey areas in anything he did.'

Time and again, McQueen's professional inner sanctum would witness their leader, crouched on his studio floor in silent concentration, single-handedly chalking out and cutting a garment in minutes. 'He could literally create a dress on the spot,' Burton said. Once he had sliced the fabric – with the focused dexterity of a real-life Edward Scissorhands – the designer would then pin it onto Polina Kasina, his fitting model of many years. Further cutting and alteration would be done organically. If a piece turned out to be complicated, he would sometimes move her around for hours, until he got it right.

McQueen's punk version of Edwardian style is playfully
captured by Patrick Demarchelier in 2005.

previous pages In the same year, McQueen's flawless
tailoring and historical romanticism come together
perfectly in these two images: a Victorian-style caped
skirt suit from the 'The Man Who Knew Too Much'
collection, photographed by Roger Dean (left) and a black
dress with acres of tulle underskirt, photographed by
Patrick Demarchelier (right).

Working at these trance-like levels of intensity, finessing every fine detail, was when McQueen produced his best work. It was also, by all accounts, when he was happiest; according to Burton he, quite simply, 'came alive' when he was cutting clothes.

'I felt as if I was in the hands of a true artist' said actress Liv Tyler of the fitting she had with him for the scarlet, corseted suit that she wore to the London premiere of *The Lord of the Rings* in 2001. Naturally more sparing in her praise, the dancer Sylvie Guillem nonetheless remembered being astonished by McQueen's technical brilliance at a costume fitting for *Eonnagata*, an improvisational dance performed at Sadler's Wells in 2008. '"It's not sinister enough", he said. "Give me some fabric, give me some scissors." And, right in front of our eyes, he cut another costume. It took about three minutes.'

One of the designer's most memorable performances was shot for photographer Nick Knight's website showstudio.com. 'We all stood in silence with our mouths open,' recalled Knight, a close friend and regular creative collaborator of McQueen's, as they watched McQueen transforming a groom's white suit, by slashing and ripping, into a bridal dress.

'I like to think of myself as a plastic surgeon with a knife', he explained of the emphasis that he continually placed on the importance of good tailoring. Through cutting, he tried, he said, 'to draw attention to our unrelenting desire for perfection.' For McQueen, his craft was always about much more than clothes; it was about conveying a message. When asked, he would never fail to imbue his work with a psychological relevance.

By the end of his life, McQueen's methods of cutting and construction had reached such astonishing levels of intricacy that Burton would have paper dolls made of each outfit because his patterns were becoming too complicated to translate into two-dimensional designs. For 'Plato's Atlantis' (2010) – the last collection that he saw through to the end – McQueen's design capabilities had become so sophisticated that, even though he was using complex, digitally engineered prints, he did all the fittings for the final garments in the real fabrics, artfully draping and cutting them without once losing continuity.

'IT'S ALMOST LIKE PUTTING ARMOUR ON A WOMAN. IT'S A VERY PSYCHOLOGICAL WAY OF DRESSING.'

ALEXANDER MCQUEEN

Clothing as armour: Regan Cameron captures McQueen's stated desire to empower the women he dressed with this one-off metallic minidress.

For all McQueen's natural brilliance, his success was also founded on determination. Ambitious, and some would say arrogant, the young McQueen had a very definite strategy. 'He was so sure of his talent that it could be intimidating,' said Plum Sykes. 'Even at the beginning, he had the attitude of a superstar.' After leaving Angels, McQueen made another calculated career jump, this time going to work for Koji Tatsuno, a London-based Japanese designer who coupled a great respect for traditional craftsmanship with a more avant-garde aesthetic. When Tatsuno became a victim of a recession in the British clothing industry, McQueen set his sights on going to work for the Italian designer, Romeo Gigli.

'There was nothing going on in London and the biggest thing at the time was Gigli,' McQueen would later recall. 'He was everywhere. I thought "This is the only person I want to work for." My sister was a travel agent. I got a flight, a one-way ticket to Milan. I was twenty years old. I walked into Romeo Gigli with the worst portfolio you've ever seen, full of costume design. They said they had nothing for me and that they'd call me if anything came up. Anyway, I was walking down the street afterwards and this girl came screaming up to me like a madwoman: "Stop, stop, stop! Romeo wants to see you. He wants to see you tomorrow. Come back."'

By his own admission, the most valuable thing McQueen learnt at Gigli was the art of self-promotion. 'He had all the attention and I wanted to know why. It had very little to do with the clothes and more to do with him as a person. Any interest in the clothes is secondary to interest in the designer. You need to know you're a good designer as well, though…if you can't design, what's the point of generating hype in the first place?'

Generating hype was an art that McQueen would go on to master; later he would say 'I suppose I'm the most successful designer in England because I know how to market myself'. He took a mischievous pleasure in controversy, turning the resulting publicity to his advantage wherever he could. 'He certainly made good copy,' said Richard Benson, former Editor of *The Face*, of a profile he ran of the designer in 1995 in which McQueen declared 'I've been called "the new

Saint-Laurent" but what the f*** does that mean?' While enjoying his provocative statements, the media were not wholly convinced of his innocence. 'Despite his seeming lack of guile, his what-you-see-is-what-you-get stance,' Alix Sharkey wrote in *The Guardian* in 1996. 'McQueen is a deft and subtle media player. He knows how easy it is, speaking his mind, to send shudders of delight and horror through the kissy-kissy world of fashion – where bitching about others is always done behind their backs.'

Certainly, McQueen was unlike anything that the fashion world had ever seen before. With his shaved head, gap-toothed smile, scruffy jeans and guttural cockney twang, he had the air of someone more likely to steal a handbag than admire it. He wasn't the first budding fashion designer to come from working-class roots – John Galliano, who had graduated from Saint Martins eight years before him, was a plumber's son from south London – but he was certainly the first to make no attempt to hide them. Slightly overweight, with a penchant for junk food and Woodpecker cider and a dirty laugh that would bubble up from nowhere, McQueen was like a breath of fresh air. And it was precisely this unique persona and the strong sense of self that he radiated – a magnetic, unapologetic bravado – that made him stand out. There might have been a shy, vulnerable soul lurking just beneath the caricature but he did not show that to the fashion world.

No one will ever know whether or not, while working at Anderson & Sheppard, McQueen stitched 'I am a c***' into the lining of one of Prince Charles' suits; he insisted that it was true. However, when the suits made for the future King during McQueen's apprenticeship were duly recalled, no evidence of such obscenities was found. Equally, no one will ever know whether or not McQueen did indeed buy a one-way ticket to Milan or whether, after a year there, as Gigli's star began to wane, he decided to up and leave one day without even so much as a goodbye. But these were good stories, and they gave him the image that he wanted.

Toile amongst the lilac:
a dress from 2006's 'Neptune'
collection. McQueen's historical
romanticism made the strongest
visual impact in the hands of
photographer Tim Walker.

'I KNOW I'M PROVOCATIVE. YOU DON'T HAVE TO LIKE IT. BUT YOU HAVE TO ACKNOWLEDGE IT.'

ALEXANDER MCQUEEN

ENFANT TERRIBLE

In 1991, MCQUEEN WENT TO SEE Bobby Hillson, founder of the Postgraduate fashion course at Central Saint Martins College in London in the hope of a job teaching pattern cutting. They didn't have one. But Hillson, impressed by his obvious talent and technical brilliance, encouraged him to enrol on the College's Masters Degree Course in Fashion Design. It was not a happy period for McQueen; for the first time in his adult life he wasn't earning his own money and was forced to move back home, where, daily, he had to negotiate the vast chasm of misunderstanding between himself and his father. He persevered nonetheless and graduated, with distinction, in 1992.

McQueen's degree collection, 'Jack the Ripper Stalks his Victims', was inspired by the famous serial killer and his prostitute victims, who sold locks of their hair to be made into love tokens. Using that as reference, McQueen stitched human hair into the lining of each piece. Victorian in inspiration, there were pink frock coats and tailored black silk jackets, with blood-red linings, which drew heavily on historical influences. Other pieces had photographs of women in compromising positions screen-printed onto them.

Late to arrive at the show was Isabella Blow, then a freelance stylist. The rest is fashion history; the woman he first disregarded as a 'nutty lady' didn't stop badgering McQueen until he had agreed to sell her the entire collection. She bought one item a month, for which she paid him £100 a week. 'He'd bring an outfit in a bin liner', she recounted. 'I'd look at it and then he'd come to the cashpoint with me.' Establishing herself as his unofficial PR, stylist and muse, Blow – who was by then working at British *Vogue* – had a new protégé. She wore his graduate collection for a self-styled fashion shoot that appeared in *Vogue* in November 1992; it was exposure unheard of for such a recent graduate.

Retrospectively, much has been made of the unlikely friendship between the aristocrat and the cockney, gifted outsiders who found, in fashion, a means of self-

Wearing a silk frock coat with a thorn print from McQueen's 1992 St Martins graduation collection, stylist Isabella Blow (photographed here by Oberto Gili for Vogue *alongside her husband, Detmar) granted her young protégé unprecedented fashion exposure.*

expression. Whatever the truth, the importance of this union, so early in his career, cannot be overestimated in the story of McQueen's rise to fame. Not only did Blow champion him, she acted as a go-between; finding a way of easing the abrasive, gap-toothed cabbie's son into the more rarefied world of fashion in a way that he didn't necessarily know how to do. It was she who allegedly suggested he drop his Christian name – Lee – in favour of his more sophisticated middle name, Alexander (although others suggest that McQueen did this for more practical reasons, as he was claiming unemployment benefit as Lee and didn't want to be found out to be working at the time). But, most crucially, she whipped up a whirlwind of interest in his brilliance. '[He is] the only designer [to make] his audiences react emotionally to a show,' she declared. 'Be it happy, sad, repelled or disgusted.'

'The most erotic part of anyone's body' – the base of the spine, according to McQueen – is revealed by his ground-breaking 'bumster' trouser; it was exhibited in all its risqué glory in his controversial 1995 'Highland Rape' collection. Photograph by Christopher Moore.

Certainly, McQueen's shows seemed to set out to provoke extreme reactions. 'I don't want to do a cocktail party,' he admitted. 'I'd rather people left my shows and vomited. I prefer extreme reactions.' With 'Nihilism' (spring/summer 1994), his second show out of college, for which clothes splattered with mud and blood were paraded past a horrified audience, McQueen began to get the reaction he wanted. 'Alexander McQueen's debut was a horror show' wrote Marion Hume in a shocked but admiring article in *The Independent*. 'McQueen, who is 24 and from London's East End, has a view that speaks of battered women, of violent lives, of grinding daily existences offset by wild, drug-enhanced nocturnal dives into clubs where the dress-code is semi-naked.' It was here, most significantly, that McQueen had introduced his 'bumster' trouser, a torso-elongating design cut outrageously low on the hip which, in its more muted, low-rise hipster variation, would dominate the way that women dressed for the best part of the next decade.

Despite the shock factor of his next two collections – 'Banshee' (autumn/winter 1994), which saw a heavily pregnant skinhead model walk down the catwalk with 'McQueen' tattooed on her head and

'The Birds' (spring/summer 1995), in which the models – reflecting the idea of roadkill – were bound in sticky tape and streaked with oily tyre marks – it was McQueen's fifth show, 'Highland Rape' (autumn/winter 1995) that really announced the arrival of fashion's most exciting new *Enfant Terrible*.

'Highland Rape' was his first show to be staged under the aegis of the British Fashion Council in its official London Fashion Week tent. Its ripped lace dresses, ravaged McQueen-clan tartans and shredded military jackets (all made from cheap remnants picked up from fabric shops by the impoverished designer) made direct reference to the brutal treatment of the Scottish Highlanders during the Clearances of the eighteenth and nineteenth centuries. 'Scotland for me is a harsh, cold and bitter place', McQueen said at the time. 'It was even worse when my great, great grandfather used to live there … I hate it when people romanticise Scotland. There's nothing romantic about its history.'

A pale blue lace dress from 'The Birds' collection (1995), as worn by Helena Christensen and photographed by Mikael Jansson, showcases the provocative designer's more whimsical side.

But what was, according to McQueen, a theatrical staging of historical cruelty, was viewed by his critics as something much more sinister. Distraught-looking models, their breasts and bottoms exposed by tattered and torn fabrics, were seen to be the victims of sexual violence. *Women's Wear Daily* described the show as 'aggressive and disturbing'. Accusations of misogyny were thrown at McQueen.

He might have set out to court controversy, but he didn't always like the consequences. Throughout his career, McQueen would rail angrily against these woman hating accusations, eventually telling a personal story that he hoped would silence his critics. As an eight year-old boy, he explained, he had witnessed a terrifying act of domestic violence, directed at one of his older sisters by her husband. 'I was this young boy and I saw this man with his hands round my sister's neck,' he described. 'I was just standing there with her two children beside me … I've seen a woman get nearly beaten to death by her husband. I know what misogyny is. Everything I've done since then was for the purpose of making women look stronger, not naïve … I want to empower women. I want people to be afraid of the women I dress.'

Viewed as sartorial armour, his designs certainly take on an extra dimension. Strong, spiky, sculpted and structured with sharp-shoulders and cinched waists, the McQueen woman boasted the strict silhouette of a dominatrix. 'When you see a woman wearing McQueen,' the designer explained, 'there's a certain hardness to the clothes that makes her look powerful. It kind of fends people off.' Over the years, as he grew more confident, and more accomplished, McQueen would increasingly offset this impenetrability with a feminine softness but, in the mid-1990s, as his star was in its ascent, the sexuality he was propagating was one of an overtly dangerous kind. Little wonder that women like Isabella Blow and Daphne Guinness – fragile creatures for whom clothing was armour – were so drawn to his designs.

The shows might not always have been well-received – 'I distinctly remember the lights coming up at the end of 'The Hunger' (spring/summer 1996) show and seeing the fashion editors shaking their heads and tutting their disapproval,' said Richard Benson. Nevertheless, McQueen's controversial performances, which always started hours late, were by now Fashion Week must-sees, with some so desperate to attend that they resorted to photocopying invitations. Time and time again, McQueen would conjure up fantastical and sinister visual worlds in which sexuality, death and transgression could collide. 'Beauty,' he declared, 'Can come from the strangest of places, even the most disgusting places.' Thus, a plastic body-formed corset with live worms trapped inside it was the standout look of 'The Hunger', and 'Dante' (autumn/winter 1996)

McQueen's 1995 'Highland Rape' collection, in which distressed-looking models wore ravaged McQueen-clan tartans, was considered 'aggressive and disturbing'. Photograph by Christopher Moore.

saw blue-blooded models like Honor Fraser and Annabelle Neilson sent down the candlelit, crucifix-shaped catwalk in the nave of Hawksmoor's Christ Church in Spitalfields with pale, expressionless faces and blue-black lips. Severe lace corsets and jackets photo-printed with images of war photographs by Don McCullin were accessorised with the sadomasochistic creations of milliner Philip Treacy and jeweller Shaun Leane – masks decorated with crucifixes and armlets made to resemble crowns of thorns.

McQueen, whose character was equally capable of sweet lightness and dark intensity ('I oscillate between life and death, happiness and sadness, good and evil'), was here revealing an early tendency to explore that duality, through fashion. Veering between transcendent joyfulness and damned desolation, *Dante* – for which its art director, Simon Costin, had strategically seated a skeleton in the front row – cemented McQueen's growing international reputation as one of Britain's most exciting young designers. Within nine months of the show, aged just 27, he had been appointed John Galliano's successor as Head Designer at the legendary Parisian couture house Givenchy.

I t was an autumn morning in 1996 and Alexander McQueen was lying in bed with his boyfriend in the small, basement flat in Hoxton Square that he was living and working in at the time, when the telephone rang. It was his PR, Trino Verkade, saying that Bernard Arnault, the Chief Executive Officer of the French luxury goods conglomerate LVMH wanted to meet him. Presuming that they wanted him to design an accessory like a handbag, or an umbrella, McQueen's response was characteristically gauche. He needed to go to the loo and would call her back.

Featuring pieces like this sleeveless lace dress, photographed by Nick Knight, McQueen's 1996 'Dante' collection earned him international acclaim, and a job offer from the house of Givenchy.

overleaf *McQueen's unmatched talent for tailoring was given its most classic airing in the work he produced at Givenchy, like this elegant silk trouser suit, photographed by Robin Derrick.*

McQueen agreed to the meeting, at which it became clear that he was being offered the top job at Givenchy (for a rumoured £1,000,000, payable over two years). For any other young, impoverished designer, with ambitions to work at the highest levels of fashion, it would have been a dream come true but, true to combative form, McQueen initially said no. 'I thought, I do what I want, not what everyone else wants me to do,' he later explained to British *Vogue*. 'He [Bernard Arnault] went mad; he said that I was his horse. So then I said 'yes' and they gave me two pounds of caviar and loads of champagne. The only problem is I don't like champagne.'

Right from the very beginning of his time in Paris, McQueen was contrary. He pointedly declined invitations to enter the Paris scene, and deliberately made controversial statements to the press.

'WHEN YOU
SEE A WOMAN
WEARING
MCQUEEN, THERE'S
A CERTAIN
HARDNESS TO THE
CLOTHES THAT
MAKES HER
LOOK POWERFUL.'

ALEXANDER MCQUEEN

'Paris couture started with Charles Worth, who was English, and it will begin again with Alexander McQueen,' he announced. 'I don't give a s**t what other French designers think of me. I'll bring French chic to Paris.'

If they were unimpressed by his attitude, the French fashion world was even less impressed by McQueen's first haute couture collection (spring/summer 1997), a Grecian fantasy, inspired by the myth of Jason and the Argonauts. Styled by Katy England (his creative director since 1994) and art directed by Simon Costin, the show featured Marcus Schenkenberg, the highest paid male model in the world at the time, who presided, Icarus-like, over the catwalk from a great height. Opening to gentle harp music, it ended in a shower of golden rain. A cast of the world's top models including Eva Herzigova and Kirsty Hume were sent down the catwalk in burnished gold leather corsets, billowing pleated white chiffon, dramatic white waist-skimming jackets with cuffs trailing on the ground and coats with collars extending above their ears. Accessorised with golden ivy, Minotaur nose rings and Philip Treacy headpieces made to look like sculpted rams' horns and Pegasus wings, they were not exactly what refined haute couture audiences were used to. What's more, they revealed slightly too much human flesh; one corset revealed a model's breast, while Kirsty Hume was sent out naked but for a pair of trousers, the attached braces barely covering her nipples.

Preparing for McQueen's debut spring/summer 1997 collection for Givenchy – a Grecian fantasy, accessorised with headpieces by Philip Treacy; photographed by William Klein.

Just as the cynics had suggested, it seemed that McQueen was going to struggle to reconcile his edgy aesthetic, not just with the concept of couture, but also with the spirit of Givenchy, a house whose hallmark was the sort of elegant 1950's femininity exhibited by its most famous muse, the actress Audrey Hepburn. While the English press declared the debut a triumph ('The God of Fashion' was the front cover of the London *Evening Standard*), the French fashion press roundly turned on it, declaring his couture unwearable and, worse, not real couture at all. 'Disappointing' concurred the American fashion newspaper *Women's Wear Daily*.

Always the first to use attack as a form of defence, McQueen was defiant. 'At the end of the day, Givenchy is 200 million light-years away from what I do', he said. 'One is London, the other is Paris. It's two different aesthetics – McQueen is about our times and Givenchy is about allure – and it's f***ing hard to be both at the same time.' Truthfully, McQueen was hurt and frightened by his first real taste of failure. 'I look at that first collection and me and Katy, we worked so hard,' he would admit in an interview some six years later. 'I was 27 years old and we were so brought down by that experience, emotionally and physically. It was a f***ing nightmare.'

Although the next five years would see him make huge inroads into understanding his new market, McQueen never really made a success of his time in Paris. The ultimate in understated elegance, the Givenchy house wasn't impressed when he sent space aliens and girls in Perspex robotic body suits (Pret-a-Porter, autumn/winter 1999) down Parisian runways. 'The only way it would have worked would have been if they had allowed me to change the whole concept of the house, to give it a new identity', McQueen declared retrospectively. 'And they never wanted me to do that.'

Back in England, meanwhile, it was a different story; with the revenues from Givenchy, McQueen could let his creativity run riot. 'He was really excited,' Sarah Burton would later recall of an early excursion to buy some studio chairs that would actually reach the pattern-cutting table. 'Because there was money coming in, and he could do things he'd never done before.'

Increasingly, McQueen's London shows became Fashion Week landmarks. They were intensely dramatic: for example, 'It's a Jungle Out There' (autumn/winter 1997) was set against a backdrop of corrugated iron covered in bullet holes; prowling around wrecked cars were predatory models with painted faces and white contact lenses, dressed in traditionally tailored pieces, sharp-angled jackets.

One jacket, most memorably, had horns seemingly growing out of its shoulder pads. There were also dresses made out of hides and leathers which displayed the designer's increasingly flawless technique. The shows were full of pyrotechnics – literally so in the case of 'Joan' (autumn/winter 1998), which featured models made to look like satanic serpents, their eyes reddened by creepy contact lenses, and in whose spectacular finale, a model wearing a red hooded catsuit was trapped inside a satanic ring of fire.

More like art installations than anything else, they never failed to shock, mystify and move. 'For me, what I do is an artistic expression that is channelled through me,' he explained. 'Fashion is just the medium.' These shows were spine-tingling, emotional spectacles. 'It was so beautiful tears ran down my face,' said *Vogue* Fashion Features Director Harriet Quick of McQueen's 'Untitled' spring/summer 1998 show (its sponsor, American Express, hadn't liked the sexual overtones of its intended title, 'Golden Shower'). It was McQueen at his most visually ambitious. For the first half, dark clothes were sent out onto a white, plexiglass catwalk made up of water-filled tanks underlit by thousands of neon tubes. After a short break, during which black ink flooded the tanks, the show resumed with white clothes on a black catwalk. Rain fell, models' makeup ran, dresses clung, Ann Peebles' song *I Can't Stand the Rain* played. 'It was melancholy and uplifting at one and the same time,' said Quick. 'I'll never forget it.'

A melding of Givenchy softness and McQueen structuring saw the designer produce some of his best work – like this beautiful mousseline draped bustier dress – for his 1998 'Untitled' collection.

overleaf Then at her popular prime, Japanese-American supermodel Devon Aoki – photographed here by Regan Cameron in a rigid mesh halterneck top from his 1999 'No. 13' collection – became something of a muse to McQueen in the late 1990s.

'You've got to know the rules to break them. That's what I'm here for, to demolish the rules but to keep the tradition.'

ALEXANDER MCQUEEN

'I THINK THERE HAS TO BE AN UNDERLYING SEXUALITY. THERE HAS TO BE A PERVERSENESS TO THE CLOTHES. THERE IS A HIDDEN AGENDA IN THE FRAGILITY OF ROMANCE.'

ALEXANDER MCQUEEN

'HE IS THE
ONLY DESIGNER
TO MAKE HIS
AUDIENCES REACT
EMOTIONALLY TO
A SHOW.'
ISABELLA BLOW

*A trapeze dress worn by Shalom
Harlow is spray-painted by two
robots from an Italian car factory
for the dramatic finale of
1999's 'No. 13'.*

But, for all their beauty, McQueen's shows were increasingly becoming critiques of the industry that couldn't get enough of them. 'There's not a lot of dignity in high fashion,' he explained of his decision to open his spring/summer 1999 show, 'No. 13' with the Paralympic athlete, Aimee Mullins (who, as an infant, had lost her legs from the knees down) in a pair of carved prosthetic wooden legs, a rigid leather bodice and a silk skirt ('So hard and strict and unrelenting,' said Mullins of the outfit. 'As life can be sometimes'). For McQueen – who famously banned Victoria 'Posh Spice' Beckham from the front row lest her presence divert attention from Mullins – it was a chance to try and change perspectives. Having recently art directed a photo shoot for *Dazed & Confused* featuring several men and women, including Mullins, who had physical disabilities, he simply wanted to show his audience that beauty comes from within. Tattooed on Alexander McQueen's upper right arm was a quote from Shakespeare's *A Midsummer Night's Dream* 'Love looks not with the eyes, but with the mind'. For him, his craft was always about much more than clothes; it was about conveying a message.

The spray-painted trapeze dress, photographed seven years later by Craig McDean for the 90th-anniversary edition (December 2006) of British Vogue; from a feature that picked iconic pieces from throughout the decades.

'You look at all the magazines and it's all about the beautiful people, all the time,' he said. 'I wouldn't swap the people I've been working with for a supermodel. I think they're all really beautiful and I just wanted them to be treated like everyone else.' For the show's spectacular finale, in which former ballerina Shalom Harlow was spray-painted yellow and black by two pre-programmed robots shipped in from an Italian car factory, McQueen's thoughts on the dehumanising commercialism at the heart of his industry were not hard to miss.

'As part of our birthday celebration,
we went in search of ... pieces that speak
unmistakably of their time.'

VOGUE

By the turn of the new Millennium, the four-year relationship between LVMH and McQueen had begun to reach an impasse. With six collections a year to put on (two for his own label and four in Paris), he was stretched and stressed. While the designer publicly dismissed the house's CEO, Arnault, as 'irrelevant', the house had begun to tire of his tricky theatrics (for his fourth haute couture collection (autumn/winter 1999) mannequins with lit plexiglass heads had taken the place of real models and McQueen himself had popped up from a trapdoor to take his bow). But, despite McQueen's stated desire to end his relationship with the house that, he said, was 'constraining his creativity', LVMH were unwilling to let him go until his contract officially ended in 2001.

In the autumn of 2000, McQueen met Domenico de Sole, the CEO of LVMH's arch-rival, the Gucci Group, at an Italian Vogue party in Monaco. 'I had come to a point where I had to make a decision about the next ten years of my life', he would later tell British *Vogue*. 'It was either go it alone and struggle – and never really have enough means to do the work – or look for a cash injection. I wanted a company with a basis in fashion, rather than perfume, the internet or straightforward acquisitions and the Gucci Group was top of that list.' According to the designer, he simply went up to de Sole and introduced himself. According to the rumours that surround the story, McQueen did much more than that, specifically asking a photographer to take a picture of him with de Sole so that Arnault would be sure to see it.

The Gucci Group's proposed deal – which saw them buying a 51% share of his company for a figure thought to be in excess of $20 million – promised McQueen the 'complete creative control' that he demanded. It also promised to make him a very rich man. Finalised in December 2000, while he was still under contract to Givenchy, it was the ultimate snub. Arnault then cancelled what was to be McQueen's last haute couture show for Givenchy (spring/summer 2001) at the eleventh hour.

Ironically, as his relationship with Bernard Arnault and LVMH began to sour, McQueen started to produce some of his best work for Givenchy – like this gold, bell-sleeved sequin dress, photographed by Arthur Elgort in 1999.

overleaf *A new softness began to appear in McQueen's designs for Givenchy, as exemplified in this blue ostrich feather dress, with pink net skirts, photographed by Mario Testino for the April 2000 issue of Vogue.*

'AT GIVENCHY, I LEARNED LIGHTNESS. I LEARNED TO SOFTEN. FOR ME, IT WAS AN EDUCATION ... WORKING IN THE ATELIER WAS FUNDAMENTAL TO MY CAREER.'

ALEXANDER MCQUEEN

Back in London, hardened by his Givenchy experience and with the Gucci money feeding his creative potential, McQueen staged his most searing attack on the fashion industry. As they took their seats for 'Voss' (spring/summer 2001), McQueen's audience were – quite literally – faced with their own reflections in the large, mirrored box which had taken seven days to construct. Individuals had to choose between looking away, watching themselves, or the intense, paranoia-inducing experience of watching others watching them. 'I wanted to make them think, "Am I actually as good as what I'm looking at?",' explained the designer. In one, artful move, McQueen had reduced observers to objects, turning their sharp scrutiny of the models back on themselves and making a comment on the objectifying nature of the journalist's gaze. As the mirrored outside of the box became two-way glass, the models inside it were revealed, trapped inside a psychiatric ward. In one particularly elaborate look, taxidermy eagles seemed to be swooping down on a terrified girl. 'The creepy idea began to sink in,' wrote fashion writer Sarah Mower, 'that we were being treated to a performance by some of the world's top models about beautiful women being driven insane by their own reflections.'

But the most dramatic coup de theatre was saved for the end of the show (which cost an estimated £70,000) as the sides of a smaller box within the main stage smashed down to reveal the fleshy, naked figure of the fetish writer Michelle Olley, lounging on a lace-covered sofa made from huge cow horns connected, via a breathing tube to the roof, her bandaged head covered in a ghostly grey pig mask, a swarm of deathly moths fluttering around her. Based on the artist Joel Peter Witkin's photograph, 'Sanatorium', it was as shocking as any image McQueen had ever produced, visually confronting the horror the larger body can instil in its beholder.

Feathering and ruffling on beautiful designs were a standout feature of McQueen's extraordinary and shockingly staged 2001 collection, 'Voss'. Photograph by Corinne Day.

'One of McQueen's greatest legacies was how he would challenge your expectations of beauty.'

ANDREW BOLTON, CURATOR OF SAVAGE BEAUTY

And yet, for all its alarming monstrosity, 'Voss' managed to rescue itself from menace with the artful beauty of the clothes; ornately embroidered kimono-style coats and figure-skimming dresses with feathered skirts, a standout scarlet feathered evening gown (as worn by Erin O'Connor) and, most memorably, a floor-length dress made entirely of razor-clam shells. It was clear that, however perverse the presentation, 'Voss' was about beauty. In their reviews, the fashion press were unanimous in their praise.

McQueen's time at Givenchy had not been wasted. It was clear to see that here was a designer who had reached new heights of skill and artistry. Each individual piece had a couture-like finish. The tailoring had always been there, but now there was an elegance, a femininity that had not necessarily existed. It was there in the intricate embroidery but, most noticeably, it was there in the subtle softening of the clothes. McQueen, who made no bones about the unhappiness of his time at Givenchy, had to admit that, in terms of his craft, his time had been very productive. 'As a tailor, I didn't totally understand softness or lightness,' he admitted. 'At Givenchy, I learned lightness. I learned to soften. For me, it was an education. As a designer, I could have left it behind. But working at Givenchy helped me learn my craft … Working in the atelier was fundamental to my career.'

A snow-covered homage to Stanley Kubrick's The Shining, *McQueen's autumn/winter 1999 show, 'The Overlook', illustrated the work of a designer who was increasingly becoming an artist. This dress with calligraphy patterns was photographed by Andrew Lamb.*

'For me, what I do is an artistic expression which is chanelled through me. Fashion is just the medium.'

ALEXANDER MCQUEEN

'THERE ISN'T ANYONE DOING
ANYTHING LIKE I DO. IT'S
TAKEN ME FIFTEEN YEARS TO
REALIZE THAT.' ALEXANDER MCQUEEN

STAR POWER

With a new couture sensibility and skill, and Gucci revenues behind him, Alexander McQueen was – like the birds he so loved – ready to take flight. 'It's romantic and it's hot sex' he declared of 'The Dance of the Twisted Bull' (spring/summer 2002), a Spanish-themed collection and his first to be presented on the more international stage of Paris Fashion Week. 'That's what makes the world go round and it's what sells clothes too.' And sell clothes it did: 400 per cent more than McQueen had ever sold before.

Back in London, the company began an aggressive expansion, relocating its headquarters from Amwell Street, EC1 to a modern, sky-lit 5-storey building on the Clerkenwell Road. The studio that had once had a slightly nonconformist, chaotic feel, now boasted a corporate polished-glass-and-aluminium slickness and an aquarium full of albino carp. 'It used to be about a bunch of eccentrics – everyone making the tea or coming up with ideas' McQueen's Creative Director Katy England said at the time. 'Now when I go into the office I'm thinking, "Who are all these people?"'

The McQueen team – and the brand that it was put into place to build – was growing; there were now accountants, production managers, and a new CEO (Sue Whiteley, former womenswear buying director of Harvey Nichols). For McQueen himself – 2 stone/13 kilos lighter, fitter, sleeker than he had ever been – the move was thrilling. He was particularly excited because now he could see the sky, Burton would later recall; contemporary classical music (particular favourites were Philip Glass and Michael Nyman) played where previously his work had been conducted in an environment of silent intensity.

Under the exacting eye of architect William Russell, five stores appeared in prime locations in New York, London's Bond Street, Milan, Las Vegas and Los Angeles over a three-year period, from 200–2005. For Russell, as it was for every single member of McQueen's creative inner sanctum, the experience of working with him was stressful. In pursuit of constant creative perfection, the hot-tempered designer

Super-stylist Katy England, McQueen's Creative Director from 1995 until his death fifteen years later, photographed by Nick Knight in the carousel-stripe fishtail wedding dress McQueen designed for her wedding to Bobby Gillespie of Primal Scream in 2006.

was never anything less than exacting. 'He can be really tough – an a***hole', Katy England told British *Vogue* at the time. 'But I just know how I feel most of the time when I'm working with him, which is good and spontaneous.' Famously, McQueen could blow from hot to cold in an instant; making someone cry one minute and feel like the centre of the universe the next.

The loyal professional 'family' that McQueen assembled around him was crucial for his success. 'They protect the name and what it stands for,' he said. 'They know how it started and they understand that it's about passion and integrity. We've all made it the success it is.' An innately private person who was slow to trust, there were very few people in McQueen's world that he was prepared to listen to. 'His mind was so free and the people around him, who protected that freedom, were so important,' said his friend, the photographer Norbert Shoerner.

'My job was to inspire him and help him achieve what he wanted to achieve,' said Katy England, the innovative stylist who first met McQueen in 1994 when he was still a fledgling designer. He had noticed her even before that, when he was at the Paris shows and still a student at Saint Martins. 'She was standing there in this second-hand nurse's coat, very severe, perfect for that time,' he would later recall. 'I thought she looked fantastic. I didn't have the guts to go up to her, though. I thought she'd be too elitist.' Several years later, after the success of his early collections, McQueen approached England and asked her to style his next show. It was a creative union that would last from 'The Birds' in 1995 until his death fifteen years later. 'We grew up together,' said England. 'There was total trust and understanding. We thought the same way. It was a bit telepathic sometimes.'

But England was by no means the only important woman in McQueen's working life. 'He was like a brother to us,' said Amie, Witton-Wallace, his head of press who started as work experience and stayed for eleven years until 2006. Without Trino Verkade, his PR Director and very first employee in 1995, there might have been no business at all. It was she who, right at the very beginning, would hustle for money (some of it from her own mother) to finance his early collections. (When, in 2010, McQueen's inconsolable housekeepers, the Garcias, discovered his body, it was Verkade and Sarah Burton who they called to his Mayfair flat.)

Sarah Burton is still haunted by memories of the early days – drafty mornings spent working in McQueen's studio in Hoxton Square, she in her coat at the cutting table, Verkade on the phone trying to keep the dream alive, McQueen's beloved bull terriers at their feet. Burton – a gentle, softly spoken middle-class girl from Cheshire – was his Head of Womenswear for thirteen years. She first met McQueen, aged 20, while she was studying print fashion at Central Saint Martins. Impressed by her skill, her tutor, Simon Ungless, a friend of McQueen's, suggested she interview for a year's placement with him in 1995. During the meeting, the most searching question the designer asked was whether or not she believed in UFOs. She worked through the year and rejoined McQueen after graduating in 1997.

As the company grew, so did Burton's influence; increasingly, McQueen would rely on her to draw down and commercialise the big ideas that swirled around his mind. The calm to his storm, Burton co-ordinated collection after collection, working hard to turn his brilliant, pure ideas into marketable realities. That she had found a way, by the end, of making paper cut-outs of his more complex designs so that they would be 'easier for him to see' says it all; Burton knew the creative workings of her mentor's mind so well that she became the only person who could translate them into realities. And he, in turn, inspired her daily with his unfettered vision and technical brilliance. 'You became addicted to him somehow,' she said. 'He was immediate, impulsive, an inspiration every day. Everything I know, I learnt from him.'

'My designing is done mainly during fittings.
I change the cut.'

ALEXANDER MCQUEEN

McQueen with one of the most important members of his professional
'family', Sarah Burton, Head of Womenswear for thirteen years and his
natural successor.

overleaf Red McQueen. A perfume flask decorated with a glass heart,
photographed by Mark Mattock (left); with the backing of the Gucci Group
the McQueen brand expanded into perfume, accessories and eyewear.
A silk chiffon micro-minidress from 2000's 'Eye' collection (right),
photographed by Nick Knight.

'HE WAS AN
INSPIRATION
EVERY DAY.
EVERYTHING
I KNOW,
I LEARNT
FROM HIM.'

SARAH BURTON

For all its high drama, McQueen's working formula was simple. 'Every collection began with a show,' Burton explains. 'To start working on designing a collection, [Lee] would first have to visualize how it would be seen.' 'I need inspiration' explained the man who used to boast that he could design a collection in a day. 'I need something to fuel my imagination and the shows are what spur me on, make me excited about what I'm doing.'

According to Sam Gainsbury, another key member of his collaborative clan who produced all his shows from *The Hunger* (spring/summer 1996) onwards, the problem was always rather more 'What am I not going to do?' than the opposite. Often, the very next day after a show, her phone would ring and it would be McQueen with an idea for the next one. "You're going to love this," he'd say. 'And we'd start all over again.' For all the high pressure he placed on her, Gainsbury also remembered never having laughed so much with another human being in her life. 'Nothing was impossible to him,' she said. 'Lee would tell me exactly what he wanted to do and we were there to realize it. It was no more complicated than that. He was a storyteller and the stories he wanted to tell weren't about a girl walking up and down a white runway.'

For McQueen, inspiration (which always had the end-show at its core) could come from just about anywhere: a handful of mussel shells he had found on Fairlight Cove, the beach nearest his beloved country house in East Sussex; a photograph in the National Geographic or Michel Frizot's seminal *A New History of Photography*; or perhaps just a mood, a feeling, a painting, an era in time, a glass surgical slide, the light on the pavement after the rain. From this point, mood boards would be covered with a wide range of research. McQueen was famous for having a memory like an elephant and would be curtly dismissive if anyone in his team tried to recycle an idea that had been used before. He was a fast, mercurial worker, who was so easily bored that friends used to joke that he suffered from Attention Deficit Disorder. He would produce more and more ideas during the course of designing a collection; after an intensive day with him, Burton might be left with a list of fifty different themes. Those dispatched to research them would be expected to come up with results the very next day. Unable to sit still, he would sometimes pull out all the fabrics, embroideries, leathers and furs that he was considering using and just sit surrounded by them, touching, feeling, draping. Always exhausting, sometimes hellish, working with McQueen was never anything less than thrilling. 'When we nailed it, we'd all be so happy,' said Sam Gainsbury. 'After that, it was plain sailing.'

With very little variation, the creative team that brought the theatrics of his shows to life remained the same – Gainsbury on production, her husband John Gosling on music (something McQueen always felt strongly about), Joseph Bennett on art direction, Dan Landin on lighting, Guido Paulo on hair and Val Garland on makeup. 'We are like a clan', Garland once said. 'You go places working with Lee. He pushes you.' 'Most of us didn't usually do fashion,' said John Gosling, whose natural arena was film, video and TV commercials. 'But McQueen's shows were special. He looked beyond fashion. He made it an event.' Early meetings headed by Katy England would take place months before the show to clarify the concept.

'I'll pace around for days doing f***-all, and then suddenly everything will click into place – the trigger might be an image, a jacket cuff, or the way Katy is wearing something. I've tried forcing the issue before and it comes up with badness.'

ALEXANDER MCQUEEN

The inevitable downside of McQueen's ambitious vision was the toll it took on the health and sanity of those he entrusted to bring it to life. 'We're running on coffee and cigarettes. We are all feeling very stressed,' Katy England wrote in a diary of work on 1997's 'It's a Jungle Out There'. 'It's strange: I never feel as if I've done enough.' In this instance, 'enough' had involved hiring a van in the middle of the night when McQueen had become angry about the collection being held up at customs at Heathrow airport, sitting in a waiting room for three hours, finally getting the clothes back at 2am and heading straight to the studio from the airport for a 4.30am start.

Moreover, this stress was occurring before the shows themselves had even taken place. These pieces of theatre could be so complex, so intricately choreographed that, more often than not, there was no time for a proper dress rehearsal before the actual event. 'Intense is an understatement,' recalls Guido Paulo of the atmosphere backstage. By all accounts, McQueen's behaviour there could be petrifying, ominously silent one minute, full of fire and brimstone the next. 'He really was an artist,' said Burton. 'He had to constantly better himself and it was just relentless.'

For Simon Costin, McQueen's great friend who art directed all of his early shows, these backstage tensions eventually became too much. After 'Untitled' (1998), the last show on which they collaborated, Costin wrote McQueen a letter saying that he couldn't go on, that the shows were getting too stressful, that McQueen's temper was too foul, that it was no longer fun. It was in Paris, while McQueen was working for Givenchy, that Costin had begun to detect a change in his usually joyful friend who would think nothing of greeting him at a party by creeping up behind him and biting him on the buttocks. Where once 'The Family', as they called themselves, had all gone to clubs and had fun to shake off the tensions of the shows, now they were seated in roped-off VIP areas, and in danger of taking themselves too seriously. 'I don't envy you now, Lee,' Costin had said to his friend one night over dinner, but McQueen had shrugged off his concern. After they parted, McQueen

Lauded as 'a powerful collection for powerful women,' buyers loved the beautiful, wearable designs such as this little black dress from McQueen's 2002 'Supercalifragilistic' collection. Photograph by Greg Kadell.

and Costin didn't speak for three years. But then, at a mutual friend's party, McQueen approached him with a contrite smile and an apology. Costin was struck by the physical change in the designer; the weight loss resulting from liposuction which, McQueen joked, had left him with three navels.

If McQueen was losing himself in the quagmire of fame and fortune, he wasn't showing it yet. His business was expanding, his collaborative relationships cementing and, despite their extravagant presentation, there was a new purity to the clothes, as if – according to Jess Cartner-Morley in *The Guardian* – 'more sunshine was being allowed into his world.'

'Supercalifragilistic' (autumn/winter 2002) featured lighting by the film director Tim Burton. Opening with a purple-cloaked model, with a hood as big as Little Red Riding Hood's, leading two wolfish hounds down the catwalk and ending with a caped and masked girl in a flowing black silk cloak, it was a powerful collection for powerful women. 'The general consensus after the show was that it was the first time anyone had actually wanted to wear McQueen rather than just enjoy the spectacle,' said Harriet Quick.

Fashion and fairytale collide as a cloaked model – 'Little Lilac Riding Hood', as McQueen said – with two wolves opened the 'Supercalifragilistic' show.

Collection after collection displayed McQueen's brilliance. Sexy pirates and birds of paradise swirled on the catwalk together in 'Irere' (spring/summer 2003), a sartorial fable in which McQueen melded history, exoticism and nature. At his follow-up autumn/winter 2003 show, 'Scanners', the audience could be heard gasping as the model Devon Aoki, wearing nothing but white boots and a white, hand-embroidered kimono with a huge billowing train, walked slowly through a wind tunnel high above them.

'Life to me is a bit of a Grimm fairy tale'

ALEXANDER MCQUEEN

'HERE WAS
A DESIGNER
WHO WOULD
PROPEL FASHION
FORWARD ON
A METEOR'S
TRAJECTORY.'

HAMISH BOWLES

'Irere' in 2003 was another dose of theatrical magic, a collection full of the stuff of fantasy. The pirate imagery (left) and the ruffled wrist details, scalloped lace edging and low-slung leather belts (right) gave a playful historical air to a 21st-century look. Photographs by Roger Dean.

previous page *A sartorial Bird of Paradise from 'Irere', as photographed in all its rainbow-coloured glory by Regan Cameron.*

McQueen's 'Scanners' collection in 2003 featured intricately nipped and tucked creations like this chequered ensemble photographed by Thomas Schenk. At the show (right), the models were sent out on what the designer described as a 'nomadic journey across the tundra', which made clothes like this immaculately detailed and embroidered dress, photographed by Roger Dean, seem reminiscent of Russian folk tales.

Norbert Schoerner's photograph
of the best-selling fur-edged
corset coat from 2003's
'Scanners' perfectly illustrates
the collection's rock'n'roll
wearability.

overleaf *The 'Scanners'
audience was overwhelmed
as Devon Aoki walked slowly
through a glass tunnel above
the catwalk with her silk, hand-
painted kimono billowing in the
freezing wind.*

His next, 'Deliverance' (spring/summer 2004), was an extraordinary show, inspired by the dance marathon in film-maker Sydney Pollack's Depression-era classic film, *They Shoot Horses, Don't They?* It was choreographed by the iconoclastic, avant-garde ballet dancer Michael Clark, and took two weeks to rehearse. Displaying sinuously beautiful thirties-inspired silhouettes, it opened and ended with the same bias-cut floor-length silver sequin dress; vibrantly perfect at first and worn by model Karen Elson, tarnished and decaying at the end when the dancer wearing it fainted dramatically on stage. At the end, the enraptured audience (including the usually imperturbable American *Vogue* editor Anna Wintour) sprang to their feet in a standing ovation.

'Deliverance' was a brilliant subversion of and tribute to red carpet glamour, McQueen celebrating the beautiful and at the same time attacking the culture of celebrity. 'I find that untouchable Hollywood glamour alienating', said the man who, time and again, would refuse to be pulled into the promotional machine, turning down requests to dress A-listers. 'I can't get sucked into that celebrity thing, because I think it's just crass', he declared. In saying this, he was probably deliberately choosing to ignore the irony of the financially beneficial consequences of his newly glamorous collections – the iconic skull scarf, one of the most paparazzi-snapped accessories of 2004, and the likes of actresses Sienna Miller, Lucy Liu, Sarah-Jessica Parker and Cameron Diaz all regularly photographed smiling on the red carpet in his designs. The more successful he was, the more intransigent Alexander McQueen became. In the face of euphoric praise for 'Deliverance', the obdurate designer simply dismissed it as: 'Someone else's idea. Sydney Pollack done that; I didn't do that. I just filled it up with clothes.' Within the next half a decade, this stubborn otherness – the refusal, inability even, to enjoy the fruits of his own labour, would start to overwhelm him but, before then, the work itself would just get better and better.

Despite his declared anti-celebrity stance, McQueen didn't have any complaints when A-listers like Cate Blanchett, photographed for Vogue *by Regan Cameron in a gown from 2005's 'The Man Who Knew Too Much', began to showcase his designs.*

overleaf *2004's 'Deliverance' featured some of McQueen's most sensual designs. While the show made reference to the Depression, the clothes themselves exuded 1930s glamour, like this gold lamé gown photographed by Tesh (left) and the feathered chiffon dress photographed by Corinne Day (right).*

'HE WAS A STORYTELLER AND THE STORIES HE WANTED TO TELL WEREN'T ABOUT A GIRL WALKING UP AND DOWN A WHITE RUNWAY.'

SAM GAINSBURY

By 2004, the McQueen machine was in full swing. Not only had he introduced a Menswear line but there were also expansions into other key brand-building areas – handbags, scarves, fragrance and eyewear. While his label would not officially go into profit until 2007, it was by this time certainly heading in the right direction. This success did not go unnoticed. When Tom Ford shocked the fashion world in November 2003 by announcing that he would not be renewing his contract to design for Gucci or Yves Saint Laurent, the name believed most likely to replace him as head of YSL, the most elevated label of them all, was McQueen's. Could such a raw, sometimes controversial talent adapt itself to the classic French brand? Saint Laurent himself certainly seemed to think so. 'He's someone who's very accomplished technically' he told *Women's Wear Daily* in January 2004, 'someone who could do a good job.'

In the end, after intense negotiations, McQueen turned down the offer to head the illustrious house, saying he'd rather concentrate on his own line. 'For a long time, I was looking for my perfect equilibrium, my mojo', McQueen admitted in an interview in 2005. 'And now I think I'm getting there. I've found my customer, my silhouette, my cut. You can hide so much behind theatrics but I don't need to do that anymore.'

A latticed chiffon animal-print dress from 2004's 'Pantheon as Lecum' collection. Photograph by Nick Knight.

previous pages *The showcasing of the best pieces from his Hitcock-inspired 'The Man Who Knew Too Much' collection in the December 2005 issue of* Vogue *illustrated a new, more classical approach. The images on pages 99–100 were styled by McQueen himself, as a film noir starring Charlotte Rampling and Mark Strong, and photographed by Paolo Roversi. Rampling's sumptuous beaded gown is later given a different look in a shoot by Carter Smith on page 101, accessorised with a light and elegant tweed jacket.*

'There isn't anyone else doing anything like I do. It's taken me fifteen years to come up with that concept as a designer, to become fully aware that what I'm doing is personal to me.'

ALEXANDER MCQUEEN

'BIRDS IN FLIGHT
FASCINATE ME. I
ADMIRE EAGLES
AND FALCONS.
I'M INSPIRED BY
A FEATHER BUT
ALSO ITS COLOUR,
ITS GRAPHICS, ITS
WEIGHTLESSNESS
AND ITS
ENGINEERING.
IT'S SO ELABORATE.
IN FACT I TRY AND
TRANSPOSE THE
BEAUTY OF A BIRD
TO WOMEN.'

ALEXANDER MCQUEEN

This elaborate feathered gown was the showstopper of the 'Pantheon as Lecum' collection. Photographed by his friend Tim Walker, modelled by his friend Erin O'Connor and referencing his love of birds, this avian-inspired photograph from the December 2004 issue of British Vogue was said to be one of McQueen's favourites.

'THE FACT WAS, ALEXANDER CREATED A NEW SILHOUETTE FOR HIS GENERATION. WHEN YOU LOOK BACK AT THE HISTORY OF FASHION, THE ONLY DESIGNERS WITH ANY LONGEVITY — FROM BALENCIAGA TO DIOR TO YVES SAINT LAURENT — ARE THE ONES WHO CREATED THEIR OWN ICONIC SHAPE.'

PLUM SYKES

This corseted chiffon carousel-striped dress from the 'It's Only a Game' collection (2005) was one of McQueen's most successful designs. Photograph by Tim Walker.

previous page Staged on a giant chessboard, 'It's Only a Game' was McQueen at his imaginative best. Here photographed by Roger Dean, the 'Queen' wears a dress and obi-style sash of lilac and silver brocade with a kimono collar and puffball-style skirt, a jacket of lilac silk faille embroidered with silk thread and a net undershirt embroidered to look like tattooing.

'MY COLLECTIONS HAVE ALWAYS BEEN AUTOBIOGRAPHICAL — I EXORCISE MY GHOSTS IN MY WORK.' ALEXANDER MCQUEEN

TRAGIC MUSE

In MAY 2007, TRAGEDY STRUCK Alexander McQueen's world. After a long battle with depression, Isabella Blow – who was also suffering from ovarian cancer – took her own life by drinking a fatal dose of weedkiller. There was speculation about her depression, with some blaming McQueen and claiming that he had financially and emotionally abandoned her in recent years. While his star had ascended, they suggested, he had forgotten who had helped it to shine so brightly in the first place. McQueen refused to comment, but he was devastated by her death. At her funeral, at Gloucester Cathedral, he sat behind Blow's husband, Detmar, utterly distraught. Blow was buried in a red-and-gold brocade McQueen dress. He had asked for a lock of her hair, which he had his great friend, the jeweller Shaun Leane, encase under glass and make into a ring. Not only had McQueen lost a fashion ally, but he had also lost an important piece of his past. After Blow's death, according to the pair's mutual friend Philip Treacy, McQueen consulted a number of psychics in an attempt to contact her. When Treacy persuaded him to meet a screenwriter who was working on the story of her life, McQueen broke down in inconsolable tears.

Two of the designer's greatest friends and collaborators together at a Vogue party: the milliner Philip Treacy and, behind him, dressed in McQueen, the stylist Isabella Blow. Photograph by Mario Testino.

To McQueen 'Issie brought a whole other realm of magic' said Simon Costin. 'In a weird way, she had a civilizing effect on Lee. He really appreciated that sort of refinement.' Blow's impeccable upper-class aesthetic appealed to McQueen. He shared – and was profoundly inspired by – her feeling for beauty and she, in turn, validated his creative vision. Her enthusiasm was vital. 'Isabella could make it all OK in an instant', said Treacy. 'She'd never say to Alexander "Nice dress", he would say "Oh my God I love it!"'

'It was the tailoring and the movement which initially drew me.'

ISABELLA BLOW

'ALEXANDER TRULY
LOVED BEAUTY AND
HAD EXQUISITE
GOOD TASTE
BUT HIS ABILITY
TO MERGE IT
INTRICATELY WITH
THE MACABRE
GAVE HIM AN
UNTOUCHABLE
EDGE IN FASHION.'

PLUM SYKES

*This iconic image, entitled
'Burning Down the House', was
taken by David LaChapelle
in 1996 (published in March
1997's 'Swinging London'
edition of* Vanity Fair). *Both are
dressed in McQueen, and Blow
wears a Philip Treacy hat.*

Even in the punk-like anti-authoritarianism of his beginnings, there had been a Britishness about McQueen's dramatic designs that had appealed to Blow. 'As a place for inspiration, it's the best place in the world' the designer would later say of his homeland and, in Isabella Blow, daughter of an upper-class military officer, wife of a society landowner, appreciator of the very finest things in life, he found a human source of inspiration that he could constantly pillage. Only a year before she died (and refuting the idea that he had somehow forgotten her), he had dedicated his critically acclaimed autumn/winter 2006 collection, 'Widows of Culloden' to Blow. The exquisitely beautiful collection featuring full skirts, sweetheart necklines and swirling embroideries mined the refined sense of an aristocratic past that he had always been so drawn to in Blow. Falcon wings, nests and feathers appeared as headpieces and crowns – the type that she herself loved to wear; they were created for the show by her other great friend, McQueen's long time and much valued collaborator Philip Treacy (it was Blow who had first brought them together).

It was in collaboration with Treacy that McQueen created his posthumous fashion homage to Blow just two years later. The invitations to 'La Dame Bleue', his spring/summer 2008 collection, depicted 'Issie' in a McQueen dress, riding up to heaven in a horse-drawn carriage. Together, McQueen and Treacy created a tribute that was as beautiful, extravagant and eccentric as Blow had been in life.

Dedicated to Isabella Blow (before she died), the highly acclaimed 'Widows of Culloden' collection of 2006 featured the kind of elegant designs and Treacy headpieces that were so characteristic of Blow.

The clothes featured pointed visual references to all that Blow had loved most about his designs: flawless tailoring, rich colour palettes and distinguishing showmanship. With the smell of her signature scent, Robert Piguet's 'Fracas' hanging in the air, models were sent down the bright, white, mood-lifting catwalk in creations Blow would have loved: constructed skirt suits accentuating tiny waists with grid-like Japanese-style belts of patent red leather, moulded leather python skin dresses and billowing psychedelic kimono gowns.

'MY MOOD WAS DARKLY ROMANTIC AT THE TIME.'

ALEXANDER MCQUEEN

A dress from 'Sarabande' (spring/summer 2007) photographed in heavenly clouds by Tim Walker. Of all his collections, this was arguably McQueen's dreamiest. Inspired by Stanley Kubrick's 18th-century-set film Barry Lyndon, it revealed the softer side of fashion's enfant terrible.

overleaf Designs from 'Sarabande' like this sheer white lace appliqué dress (left), photographed by Paolo Roversi, and the dusky petalled puffball (right) were as romantic as any that McQueen had ever created.

During his weekend retreats at the Blows' Arts & Crafts Gloucestershire home, Hilles, Blow and McQueen had indulged a mutual love of bird-watching, with Blow once organising a falconer to come and give them a private display. There were avian references throughout the show – gigantic feather collars, lightly feathered mini-dresses and some tiny feathers appliquéd onto models' faces.

Blow could have worn every one of Treacy's magical headpieces – red butterfly swarms, metal visors and spiral sweeps of chain mail – with aplomb. 'When he [McQueen] worked with Philip, he was always very respectful', said Sarah Burton of the designer and the milliner's working relationship. 'Lee would show Philip mood boards and give him key words and Philip would come up with something.' From Treacy's point of view, his collaborations with McQueen were the most creatively fulfilling of his career. 'I have worked with some of the greatest designers living' he told American Vogue at the time of McQueen's death. 'But the best experience I ever had was with Alexander McQueen. He deserved excellence because what he did was beyond talent.' Their relationship hadn't always been easy – at times they had felt like love rivals for Blow's attention – but, as time went on, and McQueen's spikiness softened, they became very close. At the end of the show, as they took their bow together, grinning broadly, Treacy and McQueen (who was dressed in a kilt and a Mickey Mouse T-shirt) epitomised the two naughty boys whom Blow had so loved.

'Issie and Alexander … were from very different backgrounds but had much in common. They both had a creative vision that was innovative and thoughtful, too. They also shared a darkness.'

DETMAR BLOW

Sitting on the front row, applauding proudly, were two of McQueen's closest friends, Daphne Guinness and Annabelle Neilson, women with distinctive styles of their own to whom he had been first introduced by Blow. She had been a patron in the old-fashioned sense of the word: from the very beginning, when Blow had invited him to live with her and her husband in their house in Chelsea's Elizabeth Street, she had encouraged him to feel a part of her world. She had been particularly determined that he should meet Guinness, the dramatically stylish but shy and softly spoken granddaughter of Diana, Lady Mosley (nee Mitford). But, at first, Guinness had resisted – 'I didn't want to be a groupie.'

McQueen's great friend and muse, the fashion icon Daphne Guinness, photographed by Michael Roberts wearing a red silk satin cloak from McQueen's 2008 collection 'The Girl Who Lived in the Tree'.

Sometime later, the meeting happened organically when McQueen saw Guinness walking across the street in a kimono and ran up to her saying 'Hi, I'm the person you didn't want to meet.' The pair went to a pub and hit it off instantly; over the years, their friendship would deepen, with Guinness becoming the perfect mannequin for his empowering designs. 'Lee was the exception, not the rule' said Guinness, who staged her own performance art tribute to McQueen on the eve of the Metropolitan Museum Ball gala by changing into a feathered gown of his design in the window of Barneys department store. 'He could do anything – he was that extraordinary.' Although he designed a number of outfits for her over the years, Guinness claims rarely to have discussed fashion with her friend. 'It was only one per cent of our time together that we talked about clothing. The other ninety-nine per cent we talked about our private lives.'

'[The cloak] is an enormous volume of fabric that is all bulleted at the neck and at the hem. But although it's duchess satin, it still appears very light … he wanted this … regality but a lightness to it.'

SARAH BURTON

It was through McQueen that Guinness was introduced to the jeweller Shaun Leane, McQueen's best friend and creative collaborator, with whom she designed a number of pieces including, most notably, a diamond encrusted armour glove. Of all McQueen's friends, Leane arguably knew him the best. Born only a month apart in 1969, they shared similar backgrounds; both were gay men who had been born into large working-class families and adored their mothers. Both liked to party. Both had a shared aesthetic; a leaning towards the spiky and the body-sculpted, though often with a subtle element of delicacy. 'I particularly like the accessory for its sadomasochistic aspect', McQueen declared of the pieces that he worked closely with Leane to create over the years – silver tusk earrings ('The Hunger', 1996), thorn arm pieces ('Dante', 1997), coiled corsets ('The Overlook', 1999) and tusk mouthpieces ('Eshu', 2000). 'You got on the train and it was a fast ride, it really was' recalls Leane of their working relationship. 'He challenged you, you see. With Lee, you knew you were doing something different.' Most of all, what Leane learned from McQueen was confidence in his own abilities. When Leane expressed a fear that he didn't have the capacity to make a life-size aluminium 'spine' corset in the form of a human skeleton for 'Untitled' (1998), McQueen's response was: 'Well Shaun, if you can make it small, you can make it big. It's as simple as that.'

Widely considered to be one of his most important collections, 'The Girl Who Lived in the Tree' saw McQueen going back to his historical roots with pieces like this military brocade jacket. Photographs (here and overleaf) by Roger Dean.

overleaf *From 'The Girl Who Lived in the Tree', a dress of ivory silk tulle worn with a jacket of red silk velvet embroidered with gold bullion and trimmed with white shearling.*

After Blow died, Leane accompanied McQueen on the trip to India that provided the inspiration for his autumn/winter 2008 collection, 'The Girl Who Lived in the Tree'. While there, McQueen would send Sarah Burton text messages in the middle of the night, describing the vibrant colours that he wanted fabrics dyed. A sartorial celebration of the history of Britain and the Empire, the collection was as beautiful as any McQueen had ever created. There were military jackets worn over full, balletic tulle skirts, black velvet dresses embroidered with diamanté snowflakes and jewel-like pieces made in ruby reds, sapphire blues, golds, silvers and ermines.

'ALEXANDER MCQUEEN HANDED HIS AUDIENCE A SELF-IMAGINED FANTASY OF CRINOLINED PRINCESSES AND BRITISH-COLONIAL ROMANCE OF SUCH BEAUTY, IT ARGUABLY SURPASSED ANYTHING HE'S ACHIEVED IN 14 YEARS.'

SARAH MOWER

'CLOTHES ... SHOULD BE STARTLING, INDIVIDUAL. WHEN YOU SEE A WOMAN IN MY CLOTHES, YOU WANT TO KNOW MORE ABOUT THEM.'

ALEXANDER MCQUEEN

A prom dress of red feathers giving way to white plumage from 'The Girl Who Lived in the Tree' photographed for Vogue by Emma Simmerton.

One dress was even made in a fabric that was a digital screen print of the Queen's face. Most compelling of all was the show's final look – a ruby-red high-collared satin cloak coat, accessorised with a sceptre-like Fabergé evening bag. As it swished off the catwalk into the shadows, the audience seemed rooted to the spot, unable to wrench themselves from the most romantic story that McQueen had ever told.

If Leane was McQueen's most important male friend, Annabelle Neilson was his closest girl friend. Born into an upper class family, Neilson earned a 'wild child' reputation when she eloped to Las Vegas in 1995 to marry her childhood sweetheart, Nathaniel Rothschild (scion of the banking dynasty), only to divorce him three years later. As she got older, and she and McQueen grew closer, he seemed to fill a void in her life. 'I was sort of married to a gay man', she has confessed since his death. 'The bubble we lived in really didn't allow a lot inside it.' In the corner of his studio, where McQueen worked, two portraits looked down on him: one, of Isabella Blow, taken by Irving Penn and the other, of Neilson, taken by Craig McDean. Round their necks, both Neilson and McQueen wore necklaces that the designer had had made: black stone hearts with their initials, L & A, encrusted on them in diamonds.

Annabelle Neilson, photographed by Lee Jenkins in March 2007 wearing a dress from McQueen's 'Sarabande' collection.

Neilson, a diminutive, wide-eyed beauty, regularly wore McQueen's clothes and wore them well: one outing in 2000 in a sheer black dress of his design which didn't leave much to the imagination has become legendary. 'Lee always liked me to wear his clothes' said Neilson, a close friend of McQueen's other mischievous and beautiful friend, Kate Moss. 'Because he said that he knew that, when they were on me, they would have an adventure.' Every year, without fail, Neilson and McQueen would go on holiday together after his autumn/winter shows to celebrate their respective March birthdays. 'It was on those trips that we went diving' she recalls. 'This was where he found inspiration for his last shows, with all those vibrant colours glowing like exotic fish at the bottom of the ocean. He saw another world deep in water, one where he was at peace.'

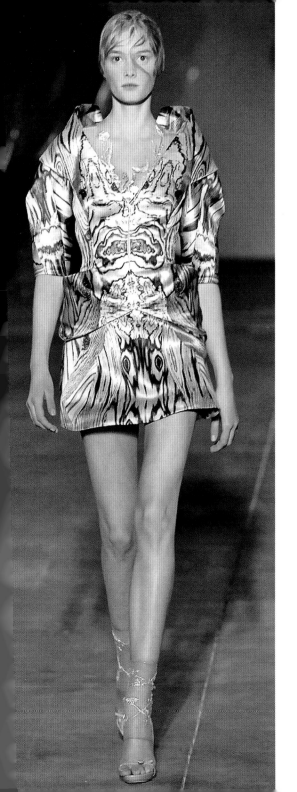

'EVOLUTION.
KEEP ON PUSHING
THE BOUNDARIES.'

ALEXANDER MCQUEEN

*Inspired by Charles Darwin's
Theory of Evolution, McQueen's
2009 collection, 'Natural
Distinction, Un-natural
Selection' saw him venture into
uncharted sartorial territory
with digitally enhanced prints
creating clothes that appeared
like living organisms or
second skins.*

For his thirty-third collection, 'Natural Distinction, Un-Natural Selection' (spring/summer 2009), McQueen sent models parading down a catwalk lined with a stuffed assortment of endangered species. 'Everything I do', the designer once declared, 'is connected to nature in one way or another.' Time and time again, McQueen would pillage the natural world for inspiration. In animals, as in birds, he was constantly drawn to 'a force, an energy, a fear that also exists in sex.'

The clothes themselves were pure McQueen – stiff minidresses with built-up shoulders, jewelled jumpsuits and angular trouser suits – but it was their fabrics that set them apart. The first of their kind, they were digitally enhanced prints that made the clothes themselves appear like living organisms; tiger stripes, vertebrae and reptile skins became the second skins of models who, with their faces covered in barely visible nylon veils, had the foetal sameness of a new breed. Sparking, as they would, a fashion for printed lycra, these thoroughly modern looks cemented McQueen's reputation as a sartorial soothsayer, a man with a passionate commitment to the evolution of fashion.

Pop's favourite fashion icon, Lady Gaga, admired McQueen so much that she reportedly felt she was channelling his spirit when writing Born This Way. *Here she is photographed in 2009 by Josh Olins wearing black from the designer's 'Horn of Plenty', the penultimate collection of his career.*

overleaf *For 'The Horn of Plenty', McQueen reworked fashion's milestones – Dior's New Look and the classic Chanel tweed suit, photographed by Patrick Demarchelier and Tim Walker respectively – into fantastic, playful parodies of themselves.*

With his final collection, it is clear to see that McQueen's imagination was entering unexplored fashion territory further than ever before. His previous collection, 'The Horn of Plenty' (autumn/winter 2009) had looked back to 1950s haute couture. 'There's no way back for me now' he said of his spring/summer 2010 collection, 'Plato's Atlantis'. 'I'm going to take you on journeys you never dreamed were possible.' Here, for all to see and for many to squirm at, was the designer's apocalyptic forecast of the impending ecological meltdown of the world. Predicting a time when, as he wrote in the programme notes, 'the ice caps would melt … the waters would rise … and life on earth would have to evolve in order to live under the sea or once more perish', 'Plato's Atlantis' was McQueen's aquatic dystopia; a world populated by weird, reptilian beings with almost nothing human about them at all.

Using the highly evolved digitised prints that he had begun to work with in his previous two collections, McQueen cemented his reputation as a man with a passionate commitment to the progress of fashion. Vibrant fabrics appeared like second skins; the perfect product of a man who loved technology. McQueen became the first fashion designer to stream one of his shows live over the internet when 'Plato's Atlantis' was broadcast on showstudio.com. When asked in an interview with Nick Knight, the creator of the site, what he still wanted to achieve in fashion, McQueen's barely audible reply was simple. 'Evolution. Keep pushing the boundaries.' The show saw the first outing of the mutant 12-inch/30-centimetre 'Armadillo' shoe made famous by Lady Gaga, whose best-selling single, *Bad Romance*, was given its first airing at the show's finale. The subject might have been the end of the world as we know it but, to all who saw it, the collection seemed to mark the beginning of a new sartorial era for McQueen. At the gathering of friends in his Paris hotel room the night after the show, Daphne Guinness remembered a thrilled McQueen. 'I have never seen him happier or so full of ideas. It was a really wonderful evening.'

However, with hindsight, it is possible to see a designer who was withdrawing from the world at the time of this last collection. Disquieting, in retrospect, was his curtain call; never one to bask in the limelight, McQueen seemed unable to even look at it, rushing gracelessly across the back of the stage with a cursory wave. And in the interview with Nick Knight, he seems pale, withdrawn and thoughtful. 'For me, Atlantis is a metaphor for Neverland' he explains, without once looking up to camera. 'It could be anywhere in your mind, anywhere that people find sanctuary in the bad times.' Within a matter of months, unable to find a sanctuary of his own, McQueen had shocked the world by taking his own life.

A dress of silk jacquard in a snakeskin design, embroidered with yellow enamel paillettes in a honeycomb pattern, from 'Plato's Atlantis'. Sarah Burton described how 'he would have an engineered print, and with that print he would place it on the form, and he would pin and construct these pieces that looked like they'd morphed out of the body themselves'.

previous pages *A model appears as a new type of futuristically evolved being, in a digital-patterned reptilian minidress and Armadillo platform boots (left). Like a limb from an amphibious alien, a sculpted platform shoe also from 'Plato's Atlantis' (right). Photographs by Jason Lloyd-Evans.*

'IT IS IMPORTANT TO LOOK AT DEATH
BECAUSE IT'S PART OF LIFE. IT'S A SAD
THING, MELANCHOLIC, BUT ROMANTIC
AT THE SAME TIME. IT IS THE END OF A
CYCLE – EVERYTHING HAS TO END. THE
CYCLE OF LIFE IS POSITIVE BECAUSE IT
MAKES ROOM FOR NEW THINGS.'

ALEXANDER MCQUEEN

VISIONARY ARTIST

ALEXANDER MCQUEEN USED TO JOKE that his mind sometimes had a mind of its own. 'I am melancholy,' he admitted in an interview in 2002. 'I like to live the deep in life. I have always felt misunderstood. Maybe there are times when I don't feel connected with the world.' The richer and more successful McQueen became, the more he seemed to withdraw. His obstinacy was still there but now it was darker, less like a display of bravado. While other designers waited dutifully backstage to meet fashion editors, McQueen would disappear within seconds. 'I find the social and political side of my work incredibly stressful', he admitted. 'I'm now in a position where I don't have to play the game so I choose not to. I visit. I don't stay.' Sightings of him at fashion parties and events became increasingly rare. McQueen simply wouldn't play the game; when American *Vogue* flew him to New York to be photographed by Irving Penn, the designer refused to leave his hotel room. There was talk of drugs, of acute loneliness and depression, of the pressures of his work in a climate of a recession but nobody – not even those closest to him – will ever know why he was driven to suicide. 'Everyone wants it to be so rock'n'roll and to say it was because of this or that', said Shaun Leane, who describes his friend as having a soul as deep and powerful as an ocean. 'But he was just such a sensitive boy.' 'He promised he would never do what Issie had done' said a devastated Annabelle Nielson, who was the last to see him before he died. 'But Lee was constantly fighting with demons; he had these highs and he had these lows.'

The only certain thing is that McQueen was struggling to face a future without his beloved mother, Joyce. The night her 40-year-old son took his life – 10th February 2010 – was the night before her funeral. Throughout his life, Joyce had been her youngest son's champion, making tea and providing sandwiches backstage at his early shows, believing in him completely when it felt like nobody else did. Philip Treacy has suspected that her death, so soon after that of Blow, left McQueen reeling from the loss of his 'two mothers', women who had loved and championed him unconditionally.

McQueen's death was a final, shocking act by a man whose career had been defined by its brilliant unpredictability. His memorial service was held in September 2010 at St Paul's Cathedral at the insistence of Annabelle Neilson, who fought doggedly against the tradition that only world leaders and royal family members should be remembered there. The cathedral was packed with friends, family and the fashion world. Neilson read Edgar Allan Poe's poem, 'Annabel Lee', a shared favourite that McQueen had had embroidered in gold thread onto a giant piece of cloth for her not long before he died. The singer Björk, with whom McQueen had regularly collaborated in the early stages of their respective careers, sang – dressed in a pair of giant angel wings – a poignant rendition of Billie Holiday's *Gloomy Sunday*; and Shaun Leane gave an address full of tales of the designer's mischievous propensity for bad behaviour. In many ways, McQueen seemed to be having the last laugh. 'You could really imagine him chuckling away in the ether' said Harriet Quick.

overleaf 'Angels and Demons' was McQueen's parting gift to the fashion world, as masterful a couture collection as any he had ever produced. The final look was a fitted high-collared jacket made of duck feathers hand-dipped in gold paint, worn over a layered tulle skirt, its top layer sprinkled with fine gold embroidery. Photograph by Tim Walker (left). A cardinal-red silk minidress, with hand-embellished gold foil embroidery above a skirt gathered like a curtain, glows in the gilded setting of the Parisian salon where the collection was shown. Photograph by Jason Lloyd-Evans (right).

His brilliance seemed to have reached its pinnacle with the collection he was working on right up until he died. It was McQueen's parting gift to the fashion world, lovingly completed by a devastated Sarah Burton and his team. Shown to limited groups of ten people at a time in a grand, gilded Parisian drawing room, *Untitled*, also known as *Angels and Demons*, (autumn/winter 2010) had sixteen pieces, all of which had been cut on the stand by the designer himself. It had the sombre feel of a requiem to a great artist; and an artist who, by taking inspiration and using images from the work of his favourite Old Masters – Hieronymus Bosch, Sandro Botticelli and Hugo van der Goes – could almost have been prophesying the death that would secure his place on the annals of art history.

'Every piece is unique, as was he', the select audience members were informed in the programme notes. This was certainly true of the

clothes: the vintage brocades, embroidered jacquards and a gold frock coat made of individually dyed gold feathers formed an other-worldly collection, as if McQueen had indeed had one eye on the afterlife. 'Weirdly, he had asked me to make a ghostly white sailing ship hat for it the last time I saw him' recalls Philip Treacy. The symbolism of the show was not lost on anyone who saw it. Crocodile skin ankle boots featured golden cherubs entwined with ivy and broken skulls for heels. Some had angel wings of gold leather reaching up the ankle. Grey layered chiffon dresses featured sepulchral digital prints of angel wings and saints raising their hands in benediction.

E ven in McQueen's ending, there was a new beginning. A week after the designer's death, the Gucci group announced that the label would continue. Although the name on everybody's lips to succeed him was Sarah Burton's, she herself was hesitant. 'I knew there was no way I could pretend to be him', she explained. 'But I just had to ask myself, what did Lee work for? For it all to just close down? I thought about what I wanted, what he would have wanted ... In the end, I decided just to get on with it: do my best.' Since succeeding her mentor, Burton has taken the core of his visionary fashion aesthetic and added her own gentle sensibility. The drama and rage have died down but the legacy remains: a fashion future built on an unforgettable past.

Opening little more than a year after his death, the Metropolitan Museum exhibition was the finest tribute imaginable to a natural-born artist whose canvas was clothes: over half a million people (many queueing around the block) saw his designs on display. His was a pure vision, an artist's vision. With his constant, determined, pushing of boundaries, McQueen was instrumental in defining how women looked at the start of the twenty-first century and giving them an armour with which to brave it.

Memento mori: Alexander McQueen photographed by Tim Walker for Vogue *in 2009, less than a year before he died; his attachment to the skull image as a symbol took on a melancholy significance after his death.*

overleaf *The designer's great friend Kate Moss, photographed by Lachlan Bailey, models a timelessly elegant black chiffon see-through McQueen gown.*

'HIS ICONIC
DESIGNS
CONSTITUTE
THE WORK
OF AN ARTIST
WHOSE MEDIUM
OF EXPRESSION
WAS FASHION.'

METROPOLITAN MUSEUM OF ART, SAVAGE BEAUTY EXHIBITION

Index

Page numbers in *italic* refer to illustrations

References

Alexander McQueen: Savage Beauty by Andrew Bolton, with
   contributions by Susannah Frankel and Tim Blanks, The
   Metropolitan Museum of Art, New York, 2011

Alexander McQueen: Genius of a Generation by Kristin Knox, A&C
   Black, 2010

Fashion at The Edge: Spectacle, Modernity and Deathliness by
   Caroline Evans, Yale University Press, 2003

Visionaries: Interviews with Fashion Designers by Susannah Frankel,
   Harry N Abrams, 2001

Gothic: Dark Glamour by Valerie Steele, Yale University Press, 2008

Picture credits

Author's acknowledgements:
I would like to thank the following people for their help, support and insight: Richard Benson, author and former editor of *The Face*, for his memories of a young McQueen, new on the scene, *Vogue*'s Fashion Features Director Harriet Quick for her sharp fashion insights and Features Director Jo Ellison for taking the time to read and advise. Thanks also to my husband, Jamie King, for shouldering the parenting load over the course of the summer holidays while I immersed myself in the weird and wonderful world of Alexander 'Lee' McQueen.

Publishing Director Jane O'Shea
Creative Director Helen Lewis
Series Editor Sarah Mitchell
Designer Nicola Davidson
Editorial Assistant Romilly Morgan
Production Director Vincent Smith
Production Controller Leonie Kellman

For *Vogue*:
Commissioning Editor Harriet Wilson
Picture Researcher Bonnie Robinson

First published in 2012 by
Quadrille Publishing Limited
Alhambra House
27–31 Charing Cross Road
London WC2H 0LS
www.quadrille.co.uk

Cataloguing in Publication Data: a catalogue record for this book is available from the British Library.

ISBN 978 1 84949 113 6

Printed in China